# CHILDREN'S AUTHORS

# WALTER DEAN MYERS

Jill C. Wheeler

Checkerboard
Library

An Imprint of Abdo Publishing
www.abdopublishing.com

**www.abdopublishing.com**

Published by Abdo Publishing, a division of ABDO, PO Box 398166, Minneapolis, Minnesota 55439. Copyright © 2015 by Abdo Consulting Group, Inc. International copyrights reserved in all countries. No part of this book may be reproduced in any form without written permission from the publisher. Checkerboard Library™ is a trademark and logo of Abdo Publishing.

Printed in the United States of America, North Mankato, Minnesota.
102014
012015

THIS BOOK CONTAINS
RECYCLED MATERIALS

Cover Photo: AP Photo/Charles Sykes
Interior Photos: Alamy p. 9; AP Photo/Charles Sykes pp. 5, 7, 13, 16, 21; iStockphoto p. 15;
    photo by Fred Stein/picture-alliance/dpa/AP Images p. 11
*Cover illustration copyright © 1995 by Fiona French from THE DRAGON TAKES A WIFE by
    Walter Dean Myers. Used by permission of Scholastic Inc.* p. 17
*Cover illustration copyright © 1998 by Jim Dietz from FALLEN ANGELS by Walter Dean Myers.
    Used by permission of Scholastic Inc.* p. 19

Series Coordinator: Bridget O'Brien
Editors: Rochelle Baltzer, Megan M. Gunderson
Art Direction: Neil Klinepier

**Library of Congress Cataloging-in-Publication Data**

Wheeler, Jill C., 1964-
  Walter Dean Myers / Jill C. Wheeler.
      pages cm. --  (Children's Authors)
  Includes bibliographical references and index.
  ISBN 978-1-62403-667-5
1.  Myers, Walter Dean, 1937-2014--Juvenile literature. 2.  Authors, American--20th century--Biography--Juvenile literature. 3.  Young adult literature--Authorship--Juvenile literature. 4. African American authors--Biography--Juvenile literature.  I. Title.
  PS3563.Y48Z93 2015
  813'.54--dc23
  [B]
                              2014025377

# CONTENTS

| | |
|---|---|
| Walter Dean Myers | 4 |
| At Home in Harlem | 6 |
| Write What You Can Say | 8 |
| Struggles in School | 10 |
| Soldier & Starving Artist | 12 |
| Editor | 14 |
| Books for the Others | 18 |
| Too Many Stories | 20 |
| Glossary | 22 |
| Websites | 23 |
| Index | 24 |

# WALTER DEAN MYERS

Walter Dean Myers was not afraid to write about subjects that make people uneasy. His more than 100 books for children and young adults address topics including gangs, drugs, and crime. They feature strong young people who **thrive** in poor **urban** neighborhoods.

Myers was African American. He grew up a **foster** child in a tough neighborhood in New York City, New York. Luckily, he discovered a love of books. This would lead to a career as an author.

Readers love Myers's books. He won the **Coretta Scott King Award** five times. He won **Newbery Honors** twice. One of Myers's most famous novels, *Monster*, became a *New York Times* best seller. It was the first book to win the **Michael L. Printz Award**.

As a child, Myers loved to go to the library. But after checking out books, he would hide them in a paper bag. He felt ashamed of having books in public.

As an author, Myers worked to see that no one felt ashamed of reading. He was committed to writing books that let all kids find stories that reflect their lives.

*Myers wrote books about characters who face the same challenges as their readers.*

# At Home in Harlem

Walter Dean Myers was born Walter Milton Myers on August 12, 1937, in Martinsburg, West Virginia. His parents were George and Mary Myers. Walter had an older sister and brother and a younger sister. He also had two older half sisters from his father's first marriage.

Walter was barely three years old when his mother died during the birth of his younger sister. This was during the **Great Depression**. George Myers struggled to make enough money to support the family.

George's first wife, Florence Brown, offered to help. Florence had married a man named Herbert Dean. They agreed that Walter's half sisters could live with them. They also offered to take Walter.

A year later, the Dean family moved to Harlem. Harlem was a mostly African-American part of New York City, New York.

Herbert worked as a handyman and a shipping clerk. Later he also worked as a janitor. Florence cleaned houses and worked in a factory that made buttons.

Walter quickly grew to love his new home. Florence helped him learn to read when he was just four years old. Herbert had dropped out of school after the third grade to work. He could not read or write. However, he spent countless hours telling Walter stories.

*Walter changed his middle name from Milton to Dean in 1972 to honor his adoptive parents.*

# Write What You Can Say

At home with the Deans, Walter developed a love of reading and a talent for telling stories. By age five, he read whatever he found at home. Sometimes it was short stories in Florence's magazines. Other times it was comic books.

Walter could read at a second grade level when he started public school. When he was in fourth grade, his first poem was published in the school yearbook. It was about his mother. He was so excited after seeing his words in print that he ran all the way home!

Though he was a good reader, Walter did not always do well in school. He had a **speech impediment**. He was often angry when people did not understand what he was saying. Other kids teased him, which led to fights. Walter was **suspended** from school more than once for fighting.

Once, in fifth grade, Walter had to sit at the back of the class because he had been in a fight. He began reading a comic book during a lesson. Mrs. Conway, his teacher, noticed. But Walter didn't get in trouble. She suggested he read something better and gave him a stack of books. He was hooked right away!

Mrs. Conway also encouraged Walter to write. She often asked her students to read aloud in class. Yet she knew Walter had trouble speaking. She suggested he write his own piece that he could read. Walter did. He made sure to avoid any words that he had a hard time saying.

*One of the books Walter's teacher gave him was* **East o' the Sun, West o' the Moon.** *He also enjoyed books such as* **The Three Musketeers, Tom Sawyer,** *and* **Robin Hood.**

# STRUGGLES IN SCHOOL

After elementary school, Walter attended a special junior high school. The school combined seventh and eighth grade into one year. After that, he **enrolled** in New York's Stuyvesant High School. Stuyvesant is a well-regarded boys' school known for its academic program.

Walter was doing better in school, but then his home life took a turn for the worse. One of his uncles was murdered. Around the same time, Florence was struggling with drinking too much alcohol. Because of these difficulties, Walter's grades dropped. He also began to skip school.

Despite Walter's problems, one of the teachers at Stuyvesant read his writing. She told him he had talent and to keep writing no matter what. Encouraged, Walter began writing every day. Sometimes, he skipped school to hang out in Central Park and write.

Walter thought about writing as a career. But, it did not seem like a good job for an African American. And, Walter's family did not have the money to send him to college. He felt there was no hope of being a writer.

Walter began spending more time on the streets of New York City. He still wrote, and he worked odd jobs. However, he became involved in handling drugs and was caught up in gang violence. Finally, Walter decided to join the US Army.

*Growing up, Walter didn't know famous poet Langston Hughes (above) lived in his neighborhood! Hughes wrote during the Harlem Renaissance, an African-American arts movement.*

# Soldier & Starving Artist

On his seventeenth birthday, Myers dropped out of high school and **enlisted** in the US Army.  He had read many poems and stories about life in the military.  His head was filled with stories of dying with honor on the battlefield.

Myers quickly learned that the real army was little like the army he had read about in books and poetry.  He was sent to radio repair school.  He also played a lot of basketball.

Three years later, Myers left the army.  He moved back in with his **foster** parents, who had moved to New Jersey.  There, Myers worked many different jobs, but he did not like them.  So, he returned to Harlem to become a professional writer.

Myers joked that this time in his life was his "starving artist period."  It was not all a joke.  He tried to survive on just two dollars a week in **unemployment pay**.  He lost 50 pounds (23 kg)!

*Myers enjoyed playing basketball throughout his life. He played plenty of it during his time at radio repair school!*

Then, Myers's life began to change. A friend suggested he take the **civil service** exam. It led to a job at the post office. And in 1960, he married Joyce Smith. They had a daughter, Karen, in 1961. Their son, Michael, was born in 1963.

However, the post office job did not last long. Myers's heart was in being an artist. He worked odd jobs during the day. At night, he played bongos with jazz musicians. Myers had some success writing and publishing jazz-based poetry. But, his marriage failed.

# EDITOR

In 1961, Myers **enrolled** in a writing class. The teacher told Myers he had talent. Myers worked on a picture book called *Where Does the Day Go?* It is about a boy who goes on a walk with his father and a group of children. In 1968, Myers entered the book in a contest for African-American writers. It won first place!

For a while, Myers attended night classes at the City University of New York. He also signed up for a writer's workshop at Columbia University. As it turned out, it was just what he needed.

John Oliver Killens led the workshop. He was a successful African-American writer. Killens knew the publishing house Bobbs-Merrill was looking for a new **acquisitions editor**. He urged Myers to apply for the job.

Columbia University is in New York City.

*Myers sometimes worked with his son Christopher (right), who is an illustrator. Together, they created many titles, including* We Are America: A Tribute From the Heart.

Myers got the job. He started working at Bobbs-Merrill in 1970. There, he began learning the publishing business. He helped other writers get published.

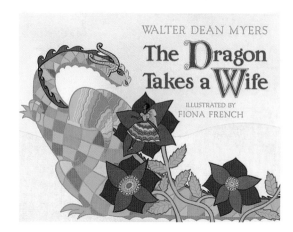

Myers continued his own writing, too. In 1972, he published another picture book. *The Dragon Takes a Wife* is the story of a lonely dragon who falls in love with a lady dragon.

Around this time, Myers also fell in love. He married Constance Brendel in 1973. They had a son, Christopher, the following year.

In 1975, Myers moved from young readers to young adult readers. He published a novel called *Fast Sam, Cool Clyde, and Stuff*. It is the story of a group of young people who deal with issues including drugs and death. Through it all, they keep a positive attitude.

In 1977, Myers left his job at Bobbs-Merrill. He decided it was a good time to do what he had always wanted to do. He became a full-time writer.

# BOOKS FOR THE OTHERS

Myers had loved to read as a child. Yet he rarely found books about people who were like him or his friends and family. Now he had time to change that.

Myers began writing books with more serious topics. The first novel he wrote as a full-time author was *It Ain't All for Nothin'*. It was published in 1978. It is the story of a boy who has to turn his father in to the police.

In 1988, Myers published *Scorpions* and *Fallen Angels*. *Scorpions* is about a young man caught up in gang violence. *Fallen Angels* is about a boy from Harlem who fights in the **Vietnam War**.

Myers said *Fallen Angels* was inspired by his younger brother, Sonny. Sonny was killed on his first day in Vietnam. Some libraries refused to carry the book because they said it talked too **vividly** about war.

In 1999, Myers wrote *Monster*. It is about a teenage boy who is arrested and tried for murder. For the book, Myers interviewed people in the law enforcement and **criminal justice** fields. He wanted to write the boy as a real person instead of as a monster.

Myers also wrote biographies. One is called *At Her Majesty's Request: An African Princess in Victorian England*. It is about a girl who is brought to live with Queen Victoria.

Myers wrote the girl's story after finding letters about her at a bookstore. He enjoyed collecting historical pictures and documents about people with African heritage. His collection inspired some of his other stories, too.

# Too Many Stories

Myers said he would never live long enough to write all the stories he had in his head.  He typically wrote five to nine pages a day, five days a week.  He worked from his home in Jersey City, New Jersey.

Myers enjoyed teaching classes and workshops, too.  He worked with students to help them write their own poems and stories.  He also told them about the importance of believing in themselves and their ideas.

In January 2012, the US Librarian of Congress named Myers the National Ambassador for Young People's Literature.  As ambassador, Myers served a two-year term to raise awareness about the importance of reading for youth.  His chosen theme in that role was "Reading Is Not Optional."

Myers promoted his theme until his death on July 1, 2014, following a brief illness.  A few months later, **grants** and the Walter Dean Myers Award were named in his honor.  They recognize authors and illustrators who celebrate **diversity** in their books. Myers's legacy will live on and inspire kids to no longer feel ashamed of reading.

*Myers never stopped writing. A graphic novel adaptation of* Monster *and other books were published after his death.*

# GLOSSARY

**acquisitions editor** - a person at a publishing company whose job is to find books for the publisher to publish.

**civil service** - the part of the government that is responsible for matters not covered by the military, the courts, or the law.

**Coretta Scott King Award** - an annual award given by the American Library Association.  It honors African-American authors and illustrators whose work reflects the African-American experience.  Runners-up are called honor books.

**criminal justice** - the systems within the government that are responsible for stopping or discouraging crime.

**diversity** - having people of different races or cultures.

**enlist** - to join the armed forces voluntarily.

**enroll** - to register, especially in order to attend a school.

**foster** - relating to a situation where a child lives with caregivers who are not his or her biological parents.

**grant** - a gift of money to be used for a special purpose.

**Great Depression** - the period from 1929 to 1942 of worldwide economic trouble.  There was little buying or selling, and many people could not find work.

**Michael L. Printz Award** - an annual award given by the American Library Association.  It recognizes the year's best young adult book.

**Newbery Honor** - an award given to a runner-up to the Newbery Medal. The Newbery Medal is an annual award given by the American Library Association. It honors the author of the best American children's book published in the previous year.

**speech impediment** - a type of disorder that affects a person's speech.

**suspend** - to be punished by being forbidden to take part in school for a set period of time.

**thrive** - to do well.

**unemployment pay** - money that the government pays to someone who is out of work to help them until they can find different work.

**urban** - of or relating to a city.

**Vietnam War** - from 1957 to 1975. A long, failed attempt by the United States to stop North Vietnam from taking over South Vietnam.

**vivid** - seeming like real life because it is clear, bright, or detailed.

# WEBSITES

To learn more about Children's Authors,
visit **booklinks.abdopublishing.com**. These links are routinely
monitored and updated to provide the most current information available.

# INDEX

**A**

*At Her Majesty's Request: An African Princess in Victorian England* 19
awards 4, 14

**B**

birth 6
Bobbs-Merrill 14, 17

**C**

childhood 4, 5, 6, 7, 8, 9, 10, 11

**D**

death 20
*Dragon Takes a Wife, The* 17

**E**

education 8, 9, 10, 12, 14

**F**

*Fallen Angels* 18
family 6, 7, 8, 10, 11, 12, 13, 17, 18
*Fast Sam, Cool Clyde, and Stuff* 17

**H**

hobbies 7, 8, 9, 12, 18, 19, 20

**I**

*It Ain't All for Nothin'* 18

**K**

Killens, John Oliver 14

**M**

military service 11, 12
*Monster* 4, 18, 19

**N**

National Ambassador for Young People's Literature 20
New Jersey 12, 20
New York 4, 6, 10, 11, 12, 14

**S**

*Scorpions* 18

**T**

teaching 20

**V**

Victoria, Queen 19
Vietnam War 18

**W**

Walter Dean Myers Award 20
West Virginia 6
*Where Does the Day Go?* 14